D1441087

STATISTICS AND PROBABILITY

STATISTICS AND PROBABILITY

EDITED BY ELISA PETERS

Britannica
Educational Publishing

IN ASSOCIATION WITH

ROSEN
EDUCATIONAL SERVICES

Published in 2015 by Britannica Educational Publishing (a trademark of Encyclopædia Britannica, Inc.) in association with The Rosen Publishing Group, Inc.
29 East 21st Street, New York, NY 10010

Distributed exclusively by Rosen Publishing.
To see additional Britannica Educational Publishing titles, go to rosenpublishing.com.

First Edition

Britannica Educational Publishing
J. E. Luebering: Director, Core Reference Group
Anthony L. Green: Editor, Compton's by Britannica

Rosen Publishing
Hope Lourie Kilcoyne: Executive Editor
Jeanne Nagle: Editor
Nelson Sá: Art Director
Nicole Russo: Designer
Cindy Reiman: Photography Manager

Introduction by John Strazzabosco.

Library of Congress Cataloging-in-Publication Data

Statistics and probability/edited by Elisa Peters.—First edition.
pages cm.—(The story of math : core principles of mathematics)
Audience: Grades 7 to 12.
Includes bibliographical references and index.
ISBN 978-1-62275-533-2 (library bound)
1. Mathematical statistics—Juvenile literature. 2. Probabilities—Juvenile literature. I. Peters, Elisa, editor.
QA276.13.S73 2015
519.5—dc23

2014030489

Manufactured in the United States of America

Cover and interior pages agsandrew/Shutterstock.com; cover (top), back cover, p. 3 (top) Indivision 07 Grow B/Getty Images.

Contents

INTRODUCTION   6

CHAPTER ONE: STATISTICAL DATA   9

CHAPTER TWO: STATISTICS AND MEASUREMENTS   23

CHAPTER THREE: STATISTICS AND VARIABILITY   38

CHAPTER FOUR: PROBABILITY   52

CONCLUSION   62
GLOSSARY   63
FOR MORE INFORMATION   65
FOR FURTHER READING   68
INDEX   70

Introduction

S tatistics and probability are two of the most useful branches of math. Statistics is the gathering, analysis, interpretation, and presentation of numerical data. Probability is the mathematical study of the chances events have of occurring. Both probability and statistics have many real-world applications. While math discoveries are fascinating in themselves, when they lead to wonderful inventions that we humans actually use, then we see why people study these ideas in the first place. For example, a major league baseball team suddenly began winning games as they never had before when they hired a statistician to find out what really was important in a game. They had found that following the same old ideas was resulting in disaster.

But perhaps even more inspiring was a recent development in the world of youth basketball that provides a glimpse into the power of statistics. A dad recently began to coach his daughter's basketball team, and strangely no one on his team could dribble or shoot the ball very well. Neither could he, for that matter. Yet they won a state championship! How? The dad studied basketball statistics and discovered a high correlation between team defense and team success. So he focused purely on

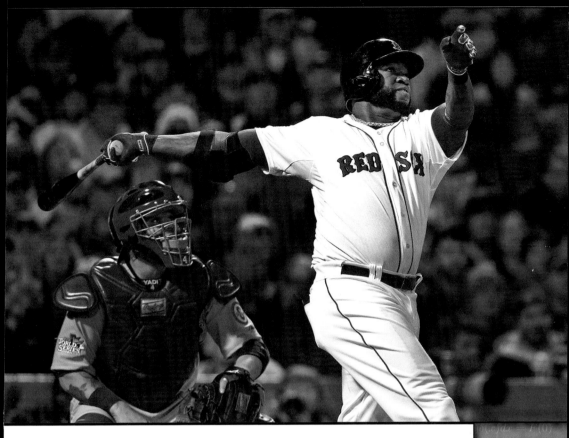

Professional baseball is a sport in which statistics plays a particularly big role. Professional statisticians work with teams, while fans can often recite their favorite players' stats. Boston Globe/Getty Images

defense. His girls scored baskets only when they stole the ball and got an easy layup. The opponents found themselves confused, frustrated, and losing to this unusual approach.

The world of probability also has fascinating uses, beyond what one might imagine. Sometimes we want to do something but have no clue about whether it's even possible.

Probability can provide clues, even to whether a situation will likely turn dangerous. For instance, when the very first astronauts were sent into space, nobody had ever done that before. One astronaut later reported that he wondered if he might get fried by light energy if he strayed outside the spaceship during a space walk. So scientists had to figure out things like what to expect from light rays and even meteorites that might shoot by out of nowhere, or many other random dangers that might occur. They were forced to have mathematicians figure out the probabilities that random problems might occur, so they might be avoided. And it worked! Our space program was successful. More important, space accidents were reduced.

STATISTICAL DATA

Anyone who watches television, browses the Internet, or reads books, newspapers, and magazines cannot help but be aware of statistics. The term *statistics* is used in two different ways. When used in the plural, it refers to numerical data. For example, one would say, "Statistics show highway accidents to be caused by . . ." When used in the singular, it means statistical methods, as in "Statistics is the body of principles and methods that has been developed for collecting, analyzing, presenting, and interpreting large masses of numerical data." Without statistical methods, there would be no way to put data together to see what they mean.

Statistics appear in the claims of advertisers, in predictions of election results and

Pie charts, like the one this businessman is using, are one common way to display statistics. © AP Images

opinion polls, in cost-of-living indexes, and in reports of business trends and cycles. Every science depends to some extent upon the gathering of data and the interpreting of the data by statistical methods. On the basis of statistics, important decisions are made in the fields of government, industry, and education. Even the average person bases many personal decisions on information that has been supplied by statisticians.

The results of statistical investigations may sometimes be stated in a single sentence, as in weather forecasting. Often, however, they are presented in the form of numerical tables or are shown pictorially in the form of graphs or charts.

HOW STATISTICAL DATA ARE COLLECTED

Statistical data are usually collected in one of the following ways: (1) by consulting existing source material, such as periodicals and newspapers, or reports from industries, government agencies, and research bureaus; (2) by setting up a survey and collecting data firsthand from individuals or organizations; and (3) by conducting scientific experiments and measuring or counting under controlled conditions.

Basic information must be collected in such a way that it is accurate, representative, and as comprehensive as possible. Statistical treatment cannot in any way improve the basic validity or accuracy of the raw data. Methods of collecting data are therefore basic to the whole field of statistics.

POPULATIONS

The term *population* ordinarily means the whole number of people in a specific place. The statistician speaks of a population of automobiles, salaries, accidents, ballots, blood pressures, or any other characteristic. For the statistician a population—also called a universe—means the entire group of items in the class being considered.

Usually it is not possible to gather observations from all the possible cases in a population. Some populations are infinite. For example,

THE LAW OF LARGE NUMBERS

In statistics, the law of large numbers is the theorem that as the number of identically distributed, randomly generated variables increases, their sample mean (average) approaches their theoretical mean.

The theorem was first proved by the Swiss mathematician Jakob Bernoulli in 1713. He and his contemporaries were developing a formal probability theory with a view toward analyzing games of chance. Bernoulli envisaged an endless sequence of repetitions of a game of pure chance with only two outcomes, a win or a loss. Labeling the probability of a win p, Bernoulli considered the fraction of times that such a game would be won in a large number of repetitions. It was commonly believed that this fraction should eventually be close to p. This is what Bernoulli proved in a precise manner by showing that as the number of repetitions increases indefinitely, the probability of this fraction being within any pre-specified distance from p approaches 1.

if you should want to count how many times "heads" will turn up when a penny is tossed, you would have to set a limit to the number of throws because even a billion would not exhaust the infinite universe of possible trials.

Here, an employee of the U.S. Census Bureau visits a household to collect information. The answers to census questions are used to measure statistically the many changes in American life. U.S. Census Bureau

Other populations, though finite, are so large that it would take too long or cost too much to collect data on each unit in them. Every ten years the United States government conducts a census of the entire population of the United States, but this is a gigantic and costly undertaking.

SAMPLES

The statistician usually gets information from a relatively small number of cases, called a sample. From the measurements or observations of the individuals sampled, generalizations can be made about the population from which the sample was selected.

The individuals in a sample must be representative of the larger population; otherwise the conclusions drawn from the sample would not be valid for the larger population. For example, one cannot draw valid conclusions about the probable outcome of a national election from interviewing a sample of 10,000 registered voters unless they are representative of the people who will actually vote in the election.

The size of the sample is also a factor. Other things being equal, a larger sample is better than a smaller one. However, excellent results can be obtained with small samples that are properly set up.

PROBABILITY SAMPLING

Statisticians use methods of sampling depending on the circumstances of the study. The basic sampling method is known as simple random sampling. It is based on probability theory. With this method, samples are drawn in such a way as to ensure that each element in the population is equally likely to be included. This is essentially what one does in shuffling and dealing a deck of cards. The dealer is simply ensuring that any card or combination of cards is equally likely to end up in one hand as it is in another. A simple random sample can be achieved by choosing the elements from a population one at a time so that each element has the same probability of being selected. However, a table of computer-generated random numbers is most often used to guarantee that each element has the same probability of being selected.

Other commonly used sampling techniques include stratified sampling, cluster sampling, and systematic sampling. All these are variations of simple random sampling. In stratified sampling, the population is divided into groups called strata. A simple random sample is selected from each stratum. The results from the strata are then combined to make generalizations about the population as a whole. Most public opinion polls are conducted on samples that are made as representative as possible by means of stratified sampling techniques. For example, a national polling sample can be set up by first dividing the whole country into various geographic areas and then dividing each area into strata according to the degree of urbanization.

Cluster sampling also involves dividing the population into groups—here called clusters. The difference is that cluster sampling uses the groups as the units of the simple random sample. One of the main applications of cluster sampling is called area sampling, where the clusters are counties, townships, city blocks, or other well-defined geographic sections of the population.

Systematic sampling includes every *nth* member of the population in the sample. For example, to study the attitudes of the subscribers to a magazine that has 10,000 subscribers, one could derive a sample of 1,000 subscribers by selecting every 10th name from a list of subscribers.

NONPROBABILITY SAMPLING

Simple random sampling and its variations are examples of probability sampling, where the probability of each unit appearing in the sample is known. In contrast, nonprobability sampling methods are based on convenience or judgment. When the population being studied is large, these methods can save time and money. Many public opinion researchers use a nonprobability sampling technique called quota sampling. The interviewers who go out to talk to people are assigned certain areas. Each interviewer is instructed to interview a specified number of people in certain categories, such as socioeconomic levels and age groups. The goal is to match the characteristics of the sample with those of the general population.

Although quota sampling can result in very accurate forecasts, it has its drawbacks. It is impossible to identify all the characteristics in the population that may affect the opinions being studied. Whether the sample is representative depends on the judgment of the people designing and conducting the survey and not necessarily on sound statistical principles. Therefore, one should be very careful in drawing conclusions about the population from quota sampling or other nonprobability methods.

Many sampling procedures are loaded in some way that may influence the results. For example, a sample of persons who volunteer for a study may not be typical of the whole group. People who send back questionnaires immediately may give different replies from those who send them back after several follow-up letters. Opinions expressed in letters to the editor on current issues would also be an example of nonrandom and nonrepresentative samples.

TWO KINDS OF DATA

The types of data that can be handled statistically occur in one of two forms. One kind is obtained by counting. The other is obtained from measurements.

DISCRETE DATA

Numbers obtained by counting a small group—such as the members of a family—are exact. If a family has three members and another child is born, the number leaps from three to four without passing through any intermediate stages, such as $3^{1}/_{2}$. A succession of such numbers is called a discrete, or discontinuous, series.

Suppose a market-research analyst wants to study consumer preferences for certain types of breakfast foods or popcorn. The researcher might ask a number of people what kinds of breakfast foods or popcorn they have on their kitchen shelves. The categories will be expressed by a word or a phrase, and the data will be an exact enumeration of the number of cases in each category. When graphed,

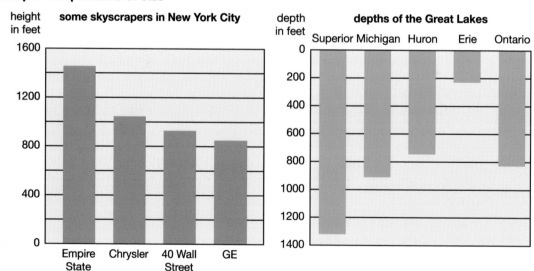

© 2014 Encyclopædia Britannica, Inc.

Bar graphs, like these, are often used to display discrete data. The left graph shows the height of four specific skyscrapers, while the right one shows the depth of each of the Great Lakes. Encyclopædia Britannica, Inc.

discrete data are usually represented by bars separated from one another to suggest the discontinuity between the categories.

CONTINUOUS DATA

The second type of data consists of measurements that fall along a continuous scale, such as distance in feet or meters, weight in pounds or kilograms, temperature in degrees, and

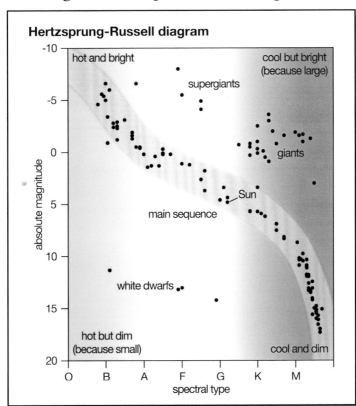

This diagram shows the relationship between how bright various stars are, how hot they are, and what kind of stars they are. This data falls along a continuous scale. Encyclopædia Britannica, Inc.

grades on tests. The measurements are usually obtained by using some sort of measuring instrument, such as a ruler, a scale, a thermometer, or a school test. This type of data is called continuous, because all gradations are possible between the lowest and highest in the series. The classes are expressed numerically and are not definite and distinct from one another.

Some types of data can be expressed as either discrete or continuous. For example, measurements of intelligence are frequently expressed in terms of "average," "above average," and "below average" instead of in numerical scores, which fall on a continuous scale. Psychological test scores are often expressed in terms of age norms or grade norms.

STATISTICS AND MEASUREMENTS

It is possible to be 100 percent accurate when counting a small group. If the numbers handled are large enough, though, errors occur. Measurements are never 100 percent accurate; there is always some residual error that cannot be eliminated. Generally, however, they are sufficiently accurate and dependable if the measuring instrument itself is accurate and the person using the instrument is a skilled observer and a careful recorder.

RELIABILITY AND VALIDITY

The reliability of a measuring instrument or of a test refers to how consistently it measures similar kinds of things, such as events or sizes of groups of people. A reliable watch will show the same time every twelve hours even though

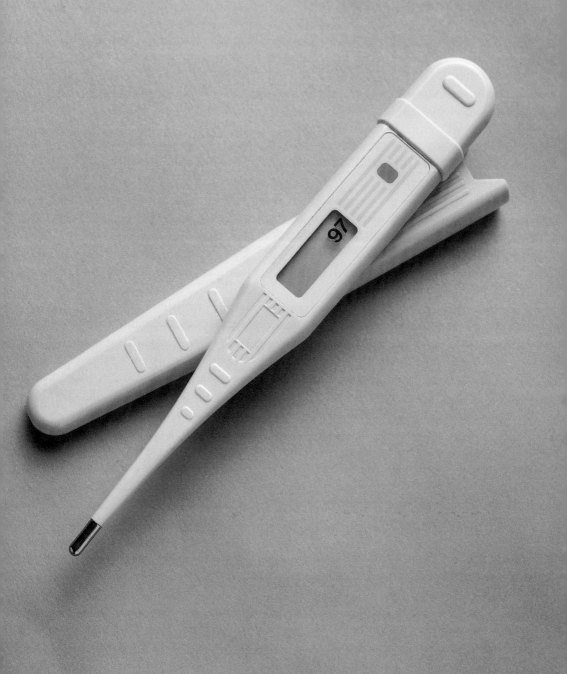

Oral thermometers, like this one, are good for measuring a person's body temperature. However, they are not valid instruments for measuring room temperature. © Al Riccio/Corbis RF

it might always be a little fast or a little slow as compared with the correct time. An accurate watch, on the other hand, gives correct time (within certain limits) according to some standard, such as Coordinated Universal Time.

The validity of a measuring instrument refers to whether or not it measures what it is supposed to measure. A thermometer is a valid instrument for measuring temperature, but one does not use it to measure humidity, wind velocity, time, or distance.

For public opinion polling, the measuring device has to be built. The measuring device that is used most often is a questionnaire. Generally it consists of a series of printed questions with spaces for writing in the answers to those questions. Poorly written questions that are difficult to understand lead to worthless information. To guard against this, a great deal of time is spent in perfecting a questionnaire before a survey is begun. The interviewers are carefully selected and are trained to secure and record the information, because they too could be a source of error. Often the interviewer conducts a small pilot study to test the questionnaire so that sources of bias and ambiguity can be removed prior to the questionnaire's use in the much larger, final survey.

FREQUENCY DISTRIBUTION TABLES

The statistician works with large masses of data. Before any conclusions can be drawn from such data, it must be condensed and arranged in usable form. Almost all tabulations that one sees are grouped in some way. One way to summarize and describe a mass of

Table I
Average Grade-Level Scores Made by a Group of 88 Sixth-Grade Students on a Standardized Reading Test (Stanford Achievement)

5.9	6.2	5.2	7.3	6.6	9.6	7.8	6.5
7.5	8.4	6.4	6.8	6.3	8.4	6.0	9.8
5.5	5.4	6.5	9.6	8.9	5.4	7.6	4.1
8.8	7.0	7.7	8.4	7.5	7.0	4.8	7.7
5.1	8.8	7.4	9.1	8.1	3.6	6.4	5.0
5.8	9.3	7.4	9.2	6.7	8.4	6.3	7.9
4.7	6.6	7.6	8.1	7.7	6.7	11.2	5.1
8.5	5.0	10.4	6.8	7.4	8.1	6.8	8.5
6.2	8.1	8.1	10.1	8.7	7.3	4.3	7.2
9.0	7.9	9.2	4.9	8.4	6.2	8.6	5.7
9.6	8.1	9.2	7.6	11.0	6.8	6.7	8.9

Encyclopædia Britannica, Inc.

statistical data is to make a frequency distribution table.

Table I lists average grade-level reading scores
made by a group of eighty-eight sixth-grade students. The scores have not been arranged in any
order. It is extremely difficult to draw any conclusions on the basis of these figures except to
say that relatively few of the sixth graders are
at a sixth-grade level (scores 6.0 to 6.9) in their
reading ability. It would be impossible, using this
haphazard arrangement, to answer readily any of
the following questions:

1. What is the range in reading ability
among these students, from highest to lowest?

2. How well do they read as a group?

3. What is the average grade-level score?

4. Do the scores seem to cluster at one or
two grade levels, or are they scattered widely?

5. What proportion is below grade level?

6. What proportion is above grade level?

7. What range of scores includes the middle half?

8. How would a pupil with a grade-level score
of, say, 6.5 compare with the rest of the group?

In order to make such data usable, the statistician ordinarily groups them into classes.

This has been done in Table II. All the possible scores, from the highest to the lowest, are written in the stub—the vertical column at the left (Grade Score).

Table II
Unit Frequency Distribution of Average Reading Scores

Grade Score	f	Grade Score	f	Grade Score	f
11.2	1	8.6	1	6.0	1
11.1		8.5	2	5.9	1
11.0	1	8.4	5	5.8	1
10.9		8.3		5.7	1
10.8		8.2		5.6	
10.7		8.1	6	5.5	1
10.6		8.0		5.4	2
10.5		7.9	2	5.3	
10.4	1	7.8	1	5.2	1
10.3		7.7	3	5.1	2
10.2		7.6	3	5.0	2
10.1	1	7.5	2	4.9	1
10.0		7.4	3	4.8	1
9.9		7.3	2	4.7	1
9.8	1	7.2	1	4.6	
9.7		7.1		4.5	
9.6	3	7.0	2	4.4	
9.5		6.9		4.3	1
9.4		6.8	4	4.2	
9.3	1	6.7	3	4.1	1
9.2	3	6.6	2	4.0	
9.1	1	6.5	2	3.9	
9.0	1	6.4	2	3.8	
8.9	2	6.3	2	3.7	
8.8	2	6.2	3	3.6	1
8.7	1	6.1			

Encyclopædia Britannica, Inc.

In the next column are tabulated the number of times each score occurs. Technically, this number is called the frequency. (In statistical work, the letter f means frequency.) The tabulating was done by taking each score shown in Table I and placing a tally mark (/) opposite that score value in Table II. The tally marks were then changed to numbers. Notice that some scores did not occur at all and others occurred more than once.

Table III is further condensed by grouping the classes to the nearest grade level. These two figures are called the class limits, and the distance between them is called the class interval. Notice that all the class intervals are the same size.

Table III
Frequency Distribution of Average Reading Scores
Tabulated to Nearest Grade Level

Score Interval	Grade Level*	f
10.5–11.4	11	2
9.5–10.4	10	6
8.5–9.4	9	14
7.5–8.4	8	22
6.5–7.4	7	19
5.5–6.4	6	12
4.5–5.4	5	10
3.5–4.4	4	3
	N =	88

*Midpoint of class interval.

One should remember that when a grouped frequency distribution is used, all information about specific individuals is lost. The unit classification in Table II is more precise, but the class interval is usually preferred because it shows more clearly the overall pattern of the group.

Table IV
Reading Status of a Group of Pupils in the Sixth Grade

Above Grade Level	63	71%
At Grade Level	12	14%
Below Grade Level	13	15%
	N = 88	

Encyclopædia Britannica, Inc.

Table IV is a summary made from Table III. It shows the data arranged in three groups according to categories that describe reading ability.

FREQUENCY DISTRIBUTION GRAPHS

Figure A shows Table III graphed in two ways. At the left is the frequency scale. Above each class interval a line is drawn on the horizontal

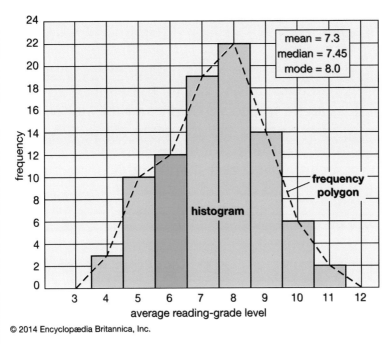

Figure A: Frequency distribution for average reading scores of 88 sixth-grade pupils to the nearest grade norm

mean = 7.3
median = 7.45
mode = 8.0

frequency polygon

histogram

frequency

average reading-grade level

© 2014 Encyclopædia Britannica, Inc.

scale at a level corresponding to the frequency of that interval. The resulting stair-step pattern is called a histogram.

Connecting the centers, or midpoints, of the class intervals by straight lines produces a frequency polygon. Notice that the frequency polygon gives the impression that the class intervals are continuous. Even a casual examination of either of these graphs, or curves, gives some idea of the general characteristics of the distribution.

CURVES

In statistics considerable attention is paid to the form of graphed curves. The distribution is said to be bilaterally symmetrical if it can be folded vertically so that the two halves of the curve are essentially the same. If the curve is lacking in symmetry, the distribution is skewed. The so-called normal curve has a bell shape and is perfectly symmetrical.

MEASURES OF AVERAGE, OR CENTRAL TENDENCY

Statisticians often seek to find some one number that will represent all the data in some definite way. One method of summarizing data is to calculate the average of the group. Statisticians use three kinds of averages. Each kind represents the group in a different way.

ARITHMETIC MEAN

The measure of central tendency most commonly used by statisticians is the same measure most people have in mind when they use the word *average*. This is the arithmetic average, which statisticians call the arithmetic mean, or simply the mean. It is obtained by adding together all the scores or values and dividing the resulting sum by the number of cases (N). In Table II the sum of the scores is 642.4. The mean is found by dividing 642.4 by 88. The resulting mean of 7.3 signifies that there were exactly enough points earned so that each pupil could have earned a score of 7.3. Because the mean is greatly affected by extreme scores, other measures of average tendency also are used.

MODE

The mode is the measure that occurs with the greatest frequency. The mode in Table II is the score 8.1 because more pupils (six) had a score of 8.1 than any other score. The mode is the only measure of central tendency that can be used with nonnumerical data. In Table IV the mode is "Above Grade Level" because more pupils (63) are in that category than are in any other category. An advantage the mode has over the other measures of central tendency is that when it exists, it is always one of the scores. For example, the mean number of children in U.S. households might be 2.5, but no household could possibly have 2.5

While the average number of pets per household in a community might be 1.3, the mode will necessarily be a whole number, such as 1. Cultura/ Getty Images

children. The mode household number of children, however, might be 2. It probably is easier to think about a typical family with 2 children than one with a statistical measure of 2.5 children.

MEDIAN

The median is defined as a value such that half of a series of scores arranged in order of magnitude are greater than the value and half are less than the value. The median is not affected by extreme scores. To find the median in the 88 cases shown in Table III, simply count down or up to the 44th and 45th cases and take the midpoint between them. This midpoint, which lies halfway between 7.4 and 7.5, is 7.45. Half of the pupils tested scored above 7.45 and half of them scored below. The typical pupil in this sixth-grade group, then, is able to read at a seventh-grade level.

Usually the measures of central tendency are near the middle of the entire distribution. As scores deviate more and more from the central tendency, they become less frequent. The median serves as a standard of comparison by means of which one can judge whether a score is common (typical) or relatively unusual (rare or atypical). In some distributions the scores or measures tend to pile up at one end or the other instead of in the middle. Such distributions are described as skewed. Other distributions appear to have more than one mode, indicating generally that two or more types of data have been included in one distribution. These distributions are described as bimodal or multimodal.

PERCENTILE RANK

The most common method of reporting results on educational and psychological tests, along with age and grade norms, is by percentile rank. Table II shows that two

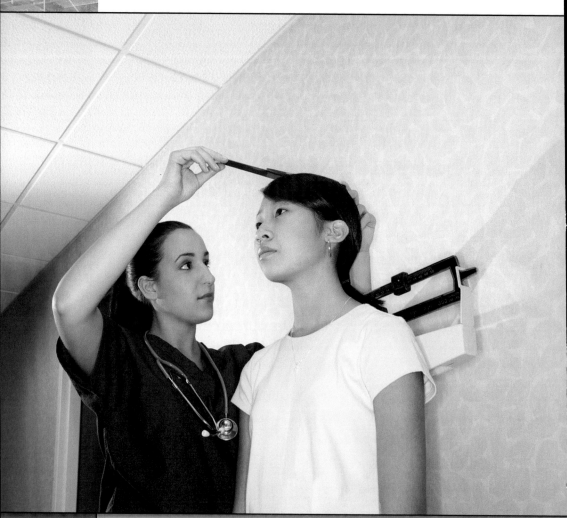

When you go to the doctor's office, the staff weighs you and measures your height. The nurse measuring you may tell you what percentile your height and weight are in. Stockbyte/Thinkstock

pupils had a score of 6.5. Because more students in the group had scores above 6.5 than had scores below 6.5, these two students are below average. Since 25 of the 88 pupils scored below 6.5, a score of 6.5 is higher than 25 divided by 88, or about 28 percent of the group. This can be expressed by stating that the percentile rank of these pupils is 28—that is, this score is higher than that made by 28 percent of the group. The median is at the 50th percentile.

3

STATISTICS AND VARIABILITY

Another element that statisticians have to pay attention to is variability, which is a measure of the spread of a data set. Let's say you are looking at the scores the students in a single grade have on a physical fitness test. It would be useful to have a way to look at how much variation there was in the scores to know if all the students had roughly the same success on the test or if there was a lot of variation in their results.

MEASURES OF VARIABILITY, OR DISPERSION

Two distributions may have averages that are exactly alike, yet there may be little or no variation in one and great variation in the other. For example, the arithmetic mean for the two distributions that follow is 4, yet in the second series the variation is zero:

Series I: 1234567
Series II: 4444444

This example shows the need for a measure that will tell whether the data cluster closely about the average or are scattered widely. Variability, like averages, is described by the statistician with a single number in order to make it easier to compare dispersions. Several measures of variability have been devised.

RANGE

The simplest measure of variability is the range—the difference between the highest and the lowest scores in the sample. In Table II the range is 7.6 grades—the distance from the highest grade level, 11.2, to the lowest, 3.6. The chief difficulty with the range as a measure of variability is that extreme scores are given too much significance.

INTERQUARTILE RANGE

When central tendency is measured by the median, percentiles may be used to indicate the spread. The interquartile range includes the middle 50 percent of the cases. It is found by determining the point below which 25 percent of the cases fall (the 25th percentile, or first quartile) and the point above which 25 percent fall (the 75th percentile, or third quartile). The difference between these two values measures the middle 50 percent of the scores or measures. In Table II the interquartile range is 2.1 (the difference between 8.4 and 6.3).

Statisticians more commonly use half this distance as their measure of variability. This is called the semi-interquartile range, or the quartile deviation. In this example it would be 1.05.

AVERAGE DEVIATION

The average, or mean, deviation is obtained by subtracting each score from the mean score and averaging the deviations—disregarding the fact that some are positive quantities and some are negative. The obtained value can be interpreted as a measure of how much the individual scores deviate, on the average, from the mean. The larger the average deviation, the greater the variability.

STANDARD DEVIATION

The best measure of variability is the standard deviation. Like the average deviation, it is based on the exact deviation of each case from the mean. The deviations, however, are squared before being added. Then the sum is divided by the number of cases and the square root is extracted. In the series of numbers 2, 4, 7, 7, 8, 9, 12, 15, 17, the mean is 9. The standard deviation is 4.6. This can be verified by performing the operation described above.

COMPARING TWO GROUPS OF SIMILAR DATA

The data presented so far consist of a single measurement for one group. Frequently it is desirable to compare two groups with regard to a single measure.

Suppose you are interested in selecting better students for a technical school with the aim of decreasing the proportion of students who fail or drop out before they finish the course. It is decided to give all entering students a mechanical aptitude test and then follow up later to see whether the test actually predicts anything about success in the school.

Table V shows the results that might have been obtained in such a study. The criterion of success is simply graduation. Before deciding to use the aptitude test for selection, however, the averages and variabilities of the two groups must be studied.

Table V
Distribution of Mechanical Aptitude Test Scores for Technical School Graduates and Nongraduates

Aptitude Scores	Frequency		
	Graduates	Non-graduates	f Combined
95–99	6		6
90–94	9		9
85–89	20	1	21
80–84	23	4	27
75–79	18	7	25
70–74	8	19	27
65–69	5	17	22
60–64	1	24	25
55–59		18	18
50–54		15	15
45–49		6	6
40–44		4	4
N =	90	115	205

Encyclopædia Britannica, Inc.

Table VI shows very clearly that the students who graduated had a higher average score than

Table VI
Summary Table Comparisons of Technical School
Graduates and Nongraduates on Aptitude Test Results

Statistical Results	Grad- uates	Non- grad- uates	Combined Group
N	90	115	205
Measures of Central Tendency:			
Mode	82	62	72, 82
Median	82.4	62.6	71.9
Mean	82.2	62.7	71.2
Measures of Variability:	(63–99)	(41–87)	(41–99)
Total Range	36	46	58
Interquartile Range	10.5	14.7	24.2
Quartile Deviation	5.3	7.3	12.1
Standard Deviation	7.8	9.8	13.2
Percentage Exceeding Mean of Total Group	90	15	

Encyclopædia Britannica, Inc.

those who did not. This is true whether one compares the modes, the medians, or the means. Note that 90 percent of graduates exceeded the mean for the total group, while only 15 percent of the nongraduates exceeded it. In addition, while there is considerable variation in each group, there is greater variability among the nongraduates than among the graduates. There is even greater variation in the combined group.

Figure B shows two simple frequency polygons on the same chart.

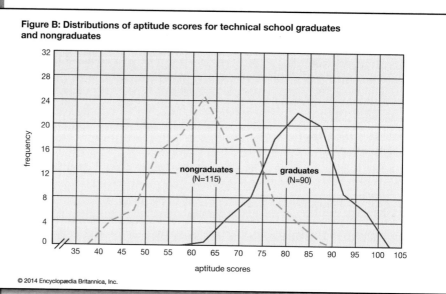

Figure B: Distributions of aptitude scores for technical school graduates and nongraduates

© 2014 Encyclopædia Britannica, Inc.

Figure C shows the two distributions in terms of cumulated percentage frequencies. The distance between the two curves shows that the graduates scored distinctly higher than did the nongraduates all along the line. Any score equivalent (such as the median score, or 50th percentile) can be obtained by running up from the percentile scale to the curve and across to the score scale. Figure C actually constitutes a set of norms for this test, because any applicant's score can be evaluated in terms of how the applicant compares with either group.

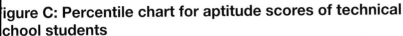

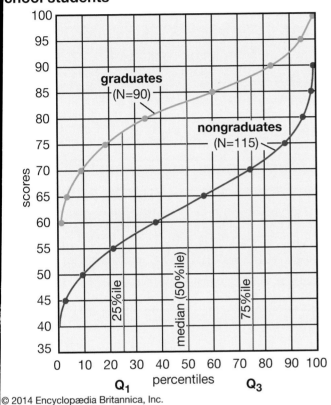

Figure C: Percentile chart for aptitude scores of technical school students

© 2014 Encyclopædia Britannica, Inc.

MEASURES OF RELATIONSHIP

When data are obtained for two or more traits on the same sample, it may be important to discover whether there is a relationship between the measures. For example, statisticians may try to answer questions such as: Is there a relationship between a person's height and weight? Can one judge a person's intelligence from any physical characteristic? Is personality related to job success? Is income related to how far a person went in school?

These questions are examples of correlation, or relationship, problems. In every case there has to be a pair of measurements for each person in the group before one can measure the correlation. For example, to determine the correlation between height and weight for high-school students, each student's height and weight must be known. By tabulating each pair of measurements on a scattergram, or scatter diagram, a visual idea of the correlation is possible.

Figure D, a scatter diagram, shows the paired grade-level scores on a test of paragraph meaning and a test of word meaning for a group of sixth-grade pupils. The vertical axis (y) is laid out in terms of grade level for the paragraph-meaning test scores. The horizontal axis (x) is laid out in terms of grade level for the word-meaning test scores. Each tally mark represents both scores for one pupil. For example, one pupil scored 8 on word meaning and 5 on paragraph meaning. The two scores are represented by a single tally mark placed

Figure D: Scatter diagram showing relationship between scores on tests of paragraph meaning and word meaning

paragraph meaning (grade scores)	4	5	6	7	8	9	10	11
11							//	//
10					₩₩ /	/	///	
9				///	₩₩ ///	//	/	
8			//	₩₩	₩₩ //	//	//	
7				//	////	/	/	
6		/	///	₩₩ ₩₩	///			
5		///	₩₩ /	/	/			
4	//	//	//					

y / x

word meaning (grade scores)

in the square that is directly above the 8 on the horizontal scale and across from the 5 on the vertical scale.

Table VII is a contingency table that shows the scores grouped by class intervals, with numerals in place of the tally marks. In both

Table VII
Contingency Table Showing the Relationship Between Grade-Level Scores on Paragraph Meaning and Word Meaning

Paragraph Meaning	Word Meaning				Total
	4–5	6–7	8–9	10–11	
10–11			7	7	14
8–9		10	19	3	32
6–7	1	15	8	1	25
4–5	7	9	1		17
Total	8	34	35	11	88

Encyclopædia Britannica, Inc.

the scatter diagram and the contingency table, the scores tend to fall into a straight band that rises from left to right. It is evident that there is a decided trend toward higher scores on paragraph meaning to go with higher scores on word meaning. This is called positive correlation. Note, however, that the correlation is not perfect. For example, ten pupils who scored at the sixth-grade level for paragraph meaning scored at the seventh-grade level for word meaning, as indicated in Figure D.

Sometimes there are negative correlations. This means that higher scores for one variable tend to be associated with lower scores for the other variable. Zero correlation indicates that there is no relationship between the two; knowing a person's score or rank on one variable would not enable the prediction of the person's score on the other variable.

CORRELATIONS AND CAUSES

High correlations—whether positive or negative—are extremely useful because they enable statisticians to make accurate predictions. Zero correlations—which will not predict anything—are also useful. They may show, for example, that one cannot judge a person's intelligence from head size. In this case the correlation between head size and intelligence is close to zero. However, a high correlation between two traits does not necessarily mean that one trait caused the other trait.

The amount of evidence required to prove a cause-effect relationship between two traits is much greater than that needed to simply show a correlation. The size of the correlation coefficient as computed for the data shown in Figure D is 0.76. Since this correlation is not extremely high, a good statistician would bear this in mind and proceed with caution in predicting one variable from the other.

Statisticians use a number called the correlation coefficient to express numerically the degree of relationship. The correlation coefficient runs from -1.00 (perfect negative correlation) through 0 (no correlation) to +1.00 (perfect positive correlation).

THE MANIPULATION
OF STATISTICS

One of the chief problems with statistics is the ability to make them say what one desires through the manipulation of numbers or

Figure E: How statistics can be misleading

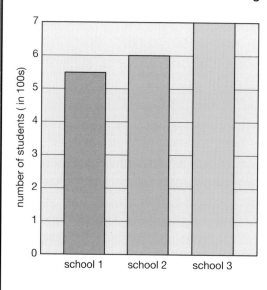

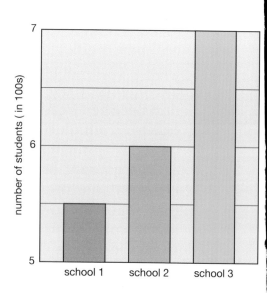

© 2014 Encyclopædia Britannica, Inc.

graphics. Graphs are frequently used in newspapers and in the business world to create a quick and dramatic impression. Sometimes the graphs used are misleading. It is up to the reader to be alert for those graphs that are designed to create a false impression. For example, changing the scales in a graph or chart or omitting a portion of the items in the sample creates a false impression. Figure E shows two graphs comparing the student populations of three schools. The second graph exaggerates the population differences by showing only the top part of the scale.

4

PROBABILITY

Hundreds of years ago mathematicians devised a way of measuring the uncertainties found in things such as games of chance. As it happens, they also created a new branch of mathematics—probability. Probability has its origin in the study of gambling and insurance in the 17th century, and it is now an indispensable tool of both social and natural sciences.

Probability is closely related to statistics since uncertainty always exists when statistical predictions are being made. There is, however, a fundamental difference between the two fields. In statistics, a sample drawn from an unknown population is used to determine what the population is like. In probability, the population is completely known; the unknown element is the likelihood of obtaining a particular sample from the population.

CHANCE AND EXPECTATIONS

Suppose two players, *A* and *B*, are playing a game where the object is to win three points. *A* has two points and *B* has one when the game is interrupted. Each player has bet 32 gold coins, for a total of 64, at the time of the interruption. How many gold coins should each receive after the interruption?

That was the question posed to mathematicians Pierre de Fermat and Blaise Pascal in 1654. Fermat gave his answer in terms of the chances, or probabilities. He reasoned that two more games would suffice in any case to determine a victory. There are four possible outcomes, each equally likely in a fair game of chance. A might win twice; first *A* then *B* might win; *B* then *A*; or *B* twice. Of these four sequences, only the last would result in a victory for *B*. Thus, the odds for *A* are 3:1, so *A* should get three times as many coins as B. That would be 48 gold coins for *A* and 16 for *B*.

Pascal proposed to solve the problem in terms of what is now called expectation. Suppose *B* had won the next round. In that case, the positions of *A* and *B* would be equal, each having won two games, and each would be entitled to 32 coins. But whereas *A* should receive his portion regardless, *B*'s share of the winnings would depend on the assumption that he had won the first round. This first round can now be treated as a fair game for this stake of 32 coins, so that each player has an expectation of 16. Hence *A*'s lot is 32 + 16, or 48, and *B*'s is just 16.

RELATIVE FREQUENCIES

The word *probability* has several meanings in ordinary conversation. One is the interpretation of probabilities as relative frequencies, for which simple games involving coins, cards, dice, and roulette wheels provide examples. The distinctive feature of games of chance is that the outcome of a given trial cannot be predicted with certainty, although the collective

People sometimes flip coins to make decisions, such as who will go first in a game, because there is no way to predict or control the outcome of a coin flip. Matt Howard/Shutterstock.com

results of a large number of trials display some regularity. For example, the statement that the probability of "heads" in tossing a coin equals one-half, according to the relative frequency interpretation, implies that in a large number of tosses the relative frequency with which "heads" actually occurs will be approximately one-half. It contains no implication concerning the outcome of any given toss.

There are many similar examples involving groups of people, molecules of a gas, genes, and so on. Actuarial statements about the life expectancy for persons of a certain age describe the collective experience of a large number of individuals but do not purport to say what will happen to any particular person. Similarly, predictions about the chance of a genetic disease occurring in a child of parents having a known genetic makeup are statements about relative frequencies of occurrence in a large number of cases but are not predictions about a given individual.

SIMPLE EXPERIMENTS

Since applications inevitably involve simplifying assumptions that focus on some features of a problem at the expense of others, it is advantageous to begin by thinking about simple experiments, such as tossing a coin or rolling dice, and later to see how these apparently frivolous investigations relate to important scientific questions.

An example of a random experiment is the tossing of a coin. The sample space consists of the two outcomes, heads or tails, and the probability assigned to each is one half. If a coin is flipped once, there are two possible outcomes—heads or tails. Since one side of the coin is as likely to turn up as the other, these outcomes are called equally likely outcomes. Probability is expressed as the ratio of favorable outcomes to the total number of equally likely outcomes. So the probability of obtaining heads is 1:2—that is, one to two, or 1/2. This probability does not mean that heads will *always* occur once in every two flips; it means that heads is *likely* to occur once in every two flips.

When a single die is rolled once, there are six possible outcomes: 1, 2, 3, 4, 5, and 6. When two dice are rolled once, there are 36 possible outcomes, as shown in the chart on page 57. A list of all possible outcomes of an experiment is called a sample space. Since five of those outcomes are the sum eight, the probability of

SAMPLE SPACE FOR A PAIR OF DICE

	1	2	3	4	5	6
1	2	3	4	5	6	7
2	3	4	5	6	7	8
3	4	5	6	7	8	9
4	5	6	7	8	9	10
5	6	7	8	9	10	11
6	7	8	9	10	11	12

This is the sample space for a pair of dice. As you can see, the combined score of the dice that you have the highest probability of rolling is seven. Encyclopædia Britannica, Inc.

rolling the sum eight is 5/36. The probability of rolling a seven is 6/36, or 1/6. (Probabilities are generally expressed in the simplest terms.)

Probabilities can be zero, one, or a number between zero and one. The probability of an impossible event is zero. Since rolling the sum 13 with two dice is impossible, its probability is 0/36, or zero. The probability of something that is certain to occur is one. Therefore, the probability of rolling a number from two through 12 is 36/36, or one.

PROBABILITY AND GENETICS

The principles of probability are widely used. Probability plays an especially important role in genetics. For example, probability is used to estimate the likelihood for brown-eyed parents to produce a blue-eyed child. In 1865, an Austrian monk, Gregor Mendel, wrote a paper that laid the foundation for modern genetics. Mendel examined seven traits that each had two distinct forms in pea plants. He first studied the inheritance of one trait at a time. This is called a monohybrid cross. To study petal color, he chose purebred purple flowers and purebred white flowers for the parental, or P, generation. When these were crossed, all of their offspring—labeled the F_1 (first filial) generation—had purple flowers. Mendel crossed the F_1 plants with each other to produce an F_2 (second filial) generation. Roughly 75 percent of the F_2 flowers had purple flowers;

the remaining 25 percent had white petals. When Mendel replicated this procedure with other traits, each cross produced the same pattern: one parental trait was expressed in all of the F1 generation and in 75 percent of the F2 generation; the remaining F2 generation displayed the nondominant trait.

Mendel analyzed his results using probability theory. He concluded that each plant had two factors for a given trait—one factor was inherited from each parent plant. Each parent had had two factors for the trait; but during reproduction the factors segregated, or separated from each other. One factor of each pair was transmitted to each offspring. Which offspring received which factor of the pair was a matter of chance. Mendel called this the principle of segregation (now also known as the law of segregation).

Today the factors Mendel described are called alleles. A pair of alleles—one from each parent—makes up a gene. The expressed characteristic of a gene (flower color, for example) is called the phenotype. The allele combination (identical alleles versus different alleles) for each trait is the genotype.

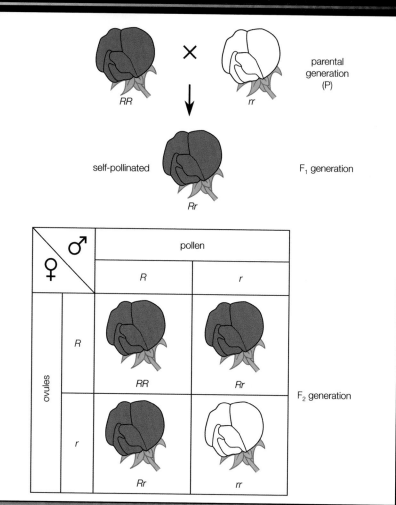

This Punnett square shows the second filial generation of Mendel's pea plants. As you can see, the F2 generation displays two phenotypes in a 3:1 ratio. Encyclopædia Britannica, Inc.

Using a grid called a Punnett square helps diagram the probability of each possible phenotype and genotype in a generation. Let R stand for the allele for purple flower color and r for the white petal allele. For many traits one allele form is dominant to the other: if the dominant allele is present, the dominant phenotype is expressed regardless of whether the second allele is the same (*RR*) or the alternative form (*Rr*). The nondominant form of the allele is called recessive. The recessive phenotype is expressed only when both alleles in the gene pair are the recessive form (*rr*).

The allele combination for each trait is the genotype. If the two alleles are alike—*RR* or *rr*—the genotype is described as homozygous. If the alleles are different—for example, *Rr*—the genotype is called heterozygous.

In a monohybrid cross beginning with a P generation of homozygous dominants (*RR*) and homozygous recessives (*rr*), all members of the F1 generation display the dominant phenotype (purple) but have a heterozygous genotype (*Rr*). A cross of two F1 individuals (*Rr* × *Rr*) produces an F2 generation composed of both dominant phenotypes and recessive phenotypes in an approximately 3:1 ratio—roughly 75 percent of the F2 will have purple flowers, and 25 percent will display white flowers. The genotypic ratio of the F2 is 1:2:1—roughly 25 percent homozygous dominant (*RR*), 50 percent heterozygous (*Rr*), and 25 percent homozygous recessive (*rr*) individuals.

Conclusion

Statistics and probability principles can have important, broad, and varied uses. You might run across a statistical term while reading an article on the prices of new homes in your area. If you have to read an academic article for a social studies, science, or even economics class, it's quite likely it will include statistical graphs and charts. If you like to read or listen to sports commentary, you're almost certain to come across a mention of probability. Probability also comes up a lot if you follow politics—particularly in regards to elections.

Whether it's basic terms (mean, median, mode) or sophisticated principles (interquartile range and standard deviation), a good understanding of statistics and probability is immensely useful. It can help you spot people who are using statistics and probability in a misleading manner and ensure that you don't mistakenly do so yourself.

analysis An explanation of the nature, meaning, or component parts of something.

arithmetic mean The average obtained by adding together all the values gathered and dividing the resulting sum by the number of cases.

average deviation A measure of variability obtained by subtracting each score from the mean score and averaging the deviations.

census The official process of counting the number of people in a country, city, or town and collecting information about them.

correlation The degree of association between two random variables.

data Facts or information used usually to calculate, analyze, or plan something. The singular of data is datum.

frequency The number of times that something happens during a particular period.

infinite Having no limits; extremely vast.

interquartile range A series of values that includes the middle 50 percent of cases.

median A value such that half of a series of scores arranged in order of magnitude are greater than the value and half are less than the value.

mode The value that occurs with the greatest frequency.

negative correlation Higher scores for one variable being associated with lower scores for another variable.

percentile rank A number between 0 and 100 that indicates the percent of cases falling at or below that score.

population A group of individual persons, objects, or items from which samples are taken for statistical measurement.

positive correlation Higher scores for one variable being associated with higher scores for another variable.

range A series of numbers that includes the highest and lowest possible amounts.

standard deviation A measure of variability obtained by squaring the deviations from the mean, adding them up, dividing by the number of cases, and finding the square root of that.

statistician A person who collects and studies statistics.

tabulation Arranging information in an organized way so that it can be studied, recorded, or so forth.

variability A measure of the spread of a data set.

American Statistical Association
732 North Washington Street
Alexandria, VA 22314
(703) 684-1221
Website: http://www.amstat.org
ASA is the world's largest organization of
    statisticians. It promotes sound statistical
    practices, as well as the development and
    spread of statistical science. Its members
    come from more than ninety countries and
    serve in a wide range of fields.

The International Statistical Institute
ISI Permanent Office
P.O. Box 24070
2490 AB The Hague
The Netherlands
Website: http://www.isi-web.org
Formally founded in 1885, the International
    Statistical Institute (ISI) promotes statistical
    research and best practices, as well as statistics
    education.

National Museum of Mathematics
11 East 26th Street
New York, NY 10010
(212) 542-0566
Website: http://momath.org

This museum is aimed particularly at children and teens. Its goal is to expand the public's understanding and appreciation of mathematics. It has exhibits and a full slate of activities to engage visitors.

Statistical and Applied Mathematical Sciences Institute
19 T.W. Alexander Drive
P.O. Box 14006
Research Triangle Park, NC 27709
(919) 685-9350
Website: http://www.samsi.info
SAMSI aims to "forge a synthesis of the statistical sciences and the applied mathematical sciences with disciplinary science."

Statistics Canada
150 Tunney's Pasture Driveway
Ottawa, ON K1A 0T6
Canada
(800) 263-1136
Website: http://www.statcan.gc.ca/start-debut -eng.html
Statistics Canada is the branch of the Canadian government that is in charge of collecting statistical data about the Canadian people. Part of its mission is to encourage sound

statistical standards and practices by operating with exemplary efficiency.

U.S. Census Bureau
4600 Silver Hill Road
Washington, DC 20233
(301) 763-4636
Website: http://www.census.gov/en.html
The U.S. Constitution requires that a count of the nation's population take place every ten years. Today, the Census Bureau conducts this census. It also collects a lot of other information about the U.S. population and is an important source of statistics about it.

WEBSITES

Because of the changing nature of Internet links, Rosen Publishing has developed an online list of websites related to the subject of this book. This site is updated regularly. Please use this link to access the list:

http://www.rosenlinks.com/TSOM/Stat

Connolly, Sean. *The Book of Perfectly Perilous Math: 24 Death-Defying Challenges for Young Mathematicians*. New York, NY: Workman Publishing Company, 2012.

Furgang, Kathy. *Understanding Economic Indicators: Predicting Future Trends in the Economy*. New York, NY: Rosen Publishing, 2012.

Gregersen, Erik. *The Britannica Guide to Statistics and Probability* (Math Explained). New York, NY: Rosen Educational Services, 2010.

Kaplan, Michael, and Ellen Kaplan. *Chances Are: Adventures in Probability*. New York, NY: Penguin Books, 2007.

Larson, Ron, and Betsy Farber. *Elementary Statistics: Picturing the World*. Upper Saddle River, NJ: Prentice Hall, 2008.

Law, Felicia. *Lightning Flash: Probability in Action* (Mandrill Mountain Math Mysteries). New York, NY: Windmill Books, 2010.

Silver, Nate. *The Signal and the Noise: Why So Many Predictions Fail—but Some Don't*. New York, NY: Penguin Press, 2012.

Takahashi, Shin. *The Manga Guide to Statistics*. San Francisco, CA: No Starch Press, 2012.

Wheelan, Charles. *Naked Statistics: Stripping the Dread from the Data*. New York, NY: W. W. Norton & Company, 2013.

Winston, Wayne L. *Mathletics: How Gamblers, Managers, and Sports Enthusiasts Use Mathematics in Baseball, Basketball, and Football*. Princeton, NJ: Princeton University Press, 2012.

Zev, Marc, Kevin Segal, and Nathan Levy. *101 Things Everyone Should Know About Math*. Washington, DC: Platypus Media, 2010.

Index

A

alleles, 59–61
analysis, 6, 9, 13, 20, 59
arithmetic mean, 32–33,
    38–39
average, measures of,
    32–35, 38
average deviation, 40, 41

B

Bernoulli, Jakob, 13

C

census, 15
chance, 6, 13, 52, 53, 54, 55, 59
   games of, 54
cluster sampling, 16, 17
contingency table, 47–48
correlations, 6, 46, 49
   coefficient, 49, 50
   negative, 49, 50
   positive, 48, 49, 50
   zero, 49
curves, 31, 32, 44

D

data, 32, 45, 49
   arrangement of, 30
   collecting, 11–12
   comparison of, 41–45

conclusions drawn
   from, 26
continuous, 21–22
discrete, 19–21
nonnumerical, 33
numerical, 6
similar, 41–44
statistical, 9, 11–13, 15–22,
   26–27
summarizing, 32
types of, 35
usable, 27
data cluster, 39
data set, 38
dispersions, 39
distributions, 30, 31, 32, 35,
   38–39, 44
   bimodal, 35
   multimodal, 35

E

errors, 23, 25
experiments, 11–12,
   55–58

F

Fermat, Pierre de, 53
frequency distribution
   graphs, 30–31
frequency distribution
   tables, 26–30
frequency polygon, 31, 44

G

genetics, 55, 58–61

I

interpretation, 6, 9, 11, 40, 54, 55
interquartile range, 39–40, 62

L

law of large numbers, 13
law of segregation, 59

M

mean, 41, 43, 62
median, 34–35, 37, 39, 43, 44, 62
Mendel, Gregor, 58–59
mode, 33–34, 35, 43, 62

N

nonprobability sampling, 18–19
    conclusions drawn from, 18–19
    techniques of, 18

P

Pascal, Blaise, 53

percentile rank, 36–37
polls, public opinion, 10–11, 17, 25
populations, 12–13, 15, 16–17, 18–19, 51, 52
    definition in statistics, 12
presentation, 6, 9, 11
probability
    definition of, 6, 54
    expression of, 56
    usefulness of, 6, 8, 62
probability sampling, 16–17
probability theory, 16, 59
Punnett square, 60

Q

questionnaire, 19, 25
quota sampling, 18–19

R

range, 27, 39–40
relationship, 45–50
    degree of, 50
relative frequencies, 54–5
reliability, 23, 25

S

sample mean, 13
samples, 15–16, 17, 18, 19, 39, 45, 51, 52

validity of, 15
sampling techniques,
  16–17, 18
scatter diagram, 46, 47–48
semi-interquartile range, 40
standard deviation, 41, 62
statisticians, 6, 11, 12, 15, 16,
  26, 27, 32–33, 38, 39, 40,
  45–46, 49, 50
  in sports, 6–7
statistics
  definition of, 6, 9
  manipulation of, 50–51

usefulness of, 6–7, 9, 11, 62
stratified sampling, 16–17
systematic sampling, 16, 17

T

tabulations, 26, 29, 46
theoretical mean, 13

V

validity, 12, 15, 23, 25
variability, 13, 38–51